Gnome Homes, A Woodsy Type of F

Later on, after getting their live yet another *interesting* idea – **Gnome Homes**! He may have reasoned that these miniature residences for gnomes might be more interesting for prospective buyers than homes for humans were. He enlisted brother Lloyd for this project also.

By using familiar outdoor materials plus lots of imagination, they constructed several of these homes, with doors, windows, swings, steps, even little gnomes or dragons in the doorways. To encourage sales, Josh came up with stories about each one, including names of gnome residents. Family members are enjoying some of these now, as buyers weren't quite as taken with the idea as Josh and Lloyd were. However, for a time it was a fun hobby and a great way to spend time together.

The Best of Senior Living

Once the kids had grown, married and left home, Josh and Annie moved away from the traffic and hassles of the metro area and joined an "active adult" community in Canton, GA. They settled into their brand-new home and instantly knew this was where they wanted to spend their retirement. Josh continues to write, publish more books, and teach. He published his first solo novel, **Resurrection Blues**, in 2011 and went on to write four humorous textbooks that he uses in his classes. In addition to the textbooks, he has published 20 novels, six short story collections, and a collaboration with his grandson Nick that came out in December, 2024.

Josh continues to share what he has learned about writing with others, conducting classes on fiction writing, memoir writing, and independent publishing. He currently teaches at Kennesaw State University in a program operating nationally called the Osher Lifelong Learning Institute.

New Writer in the Family

Recently, while vacationing with his daughter Amanda and her family, Josh's 11-year-old grandson Nick asked him if they could write a story together.

"What kind of story?" Josh asked.

Nick said, "Let's write about a battle between a gorilla and an orangutan."

Though quite used to writing about strange things, Josh replied, "I'll give it a try provided we agree to make the story as interesting as possible."

Nick agreed and they jumped into the project. Afterward, Josh said "I never dreamed we'd have so much fun. In all honesty, I experienced more sheer joy working with Nick on this than I've known when writing on ANY other story I've done."[1]

They went on to write a three-part story that appeared on Josh's blog and which will soon be available from Amazon in paperback. Josh described their experience as "A collaboration – two writers only 63 years apart!"

Josh's Bookshelf

Josh continues to write, whether he's teaching, traveling, even playing with his grandkids–he's thinking about his current project or the one he's planning next. Here are the covers from some of his recent books:

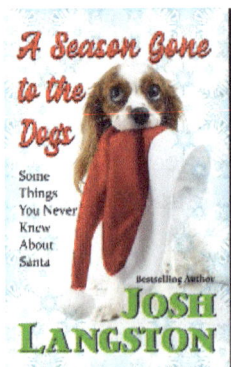

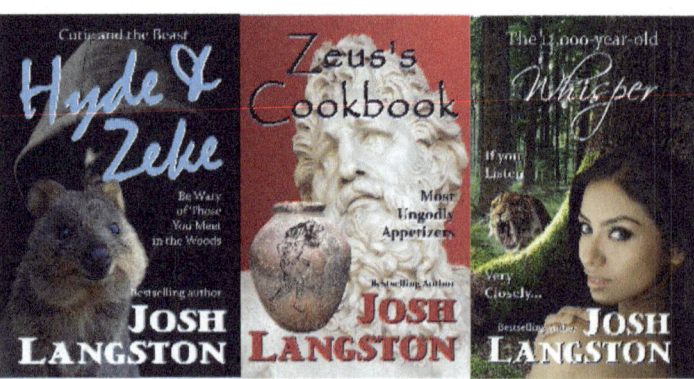

[1] From Josh Langston's Sage of the South blog

A Collaboration of Skills

Several weeks prior to Amanda and Marc's wedding, Josh and Annie decided to create a special cookbook for them. They got to work, invited friends and family to contribute their favorite recipes plus anecdotes if they wished.

The response was stunning, and the result was a 120-page creation on 8.5 x 11 pages tucked into a three-ring binder. Each page was artistically done, like a scrapbook page, with photos, text and recipes. Josh and Annie had their own recipes of course, including his Secret Meat Marinade, which nephew Dave Boyce says was the best he'd ever had.

A Growing Family

From left back row: Annabell (Bella), Lyndsay, Annie, Alexis (Lexi), Josh, Brett and Amanda. Front row: Nicholas (Nick), Knox, and Adam

Family Update

Brett and **Lyndsay** received their dental degrees while in the Army. Brett has a degree in a special field, prosthodontics. Lyndsay also has a specialty in periodontics. They have three children: **Lexi**, 18 and a freshman at the University of Georgia; **Bella**, 14, in 9th grade, and **Knox**, age 8 and in 4th grade. They currently live in Dunwoody, GA.

Amanda is still working at the Oregon State Hospital where she helps mentally-challenged adults, focusing on transitioning them to halfway homes. Her husband **Marc** works from home in consulting. They have two sons; **Nick** is 12 and in 6th grade and **Adam** is 8 who is in 3rd grade. Their family currently lives in Beaverton, OR.

Another Poem from Pop

Balloon Thank You to Josh and Family
By Wayne A. Langston

To Joshismo, Annie,
Amanda, and Brett.
It's nice to have young'uns
Who seldom forget!

I speak of the "items"
That came to my door,
So thoughtfully sent
By your family of four.

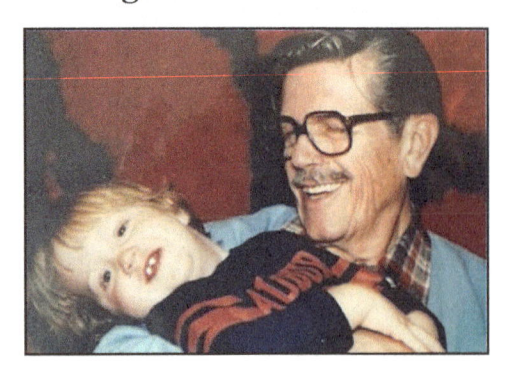

I was there in my office,
Or better still, den
When the weaver popped by
Like a turned-on hen!

"Hey! How 'bout this?"
She said with emotion,
And I instantly saw just
Why the commotion.

One balloon, two balloons
Eight balloons high!
Reached for the ceiling
Right in front of my eye!

"Get well now, y'heah?"
Was the thought each expressed.
And it truly was cheering!
Each balloon said it best.

So thank you, dear young'uns,
Thank you so much!
For a most thoughtful gesture
With a real loving touch.

And then there's Foster, another family member

As the eldest and youngest in our family, we two had a special connection. When we were younger, I helped to look after him and over the years we continued that special bond.

Our mutual interest in writing has resulted in our collaboration on this book and the previous one, *The Grandma Book*, and I have learned much from him. He is a warm-hearted guy who teaches with a relaxed, interested manner that immediately puts one at ease, as I am sure his students would agree. He is also a great family guy, and we all love him.

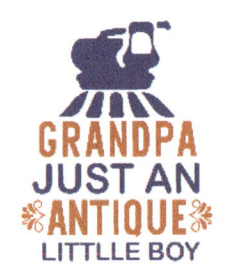

GRANDPA
JUST AN ANTIQUE
LITTLLE BOY

Chapter Six – Horace Ayres Langston, Sr
4/25/1887 – 12/29/1952

Since I was only 11 when my Grandpa Langston passed away my memories of him are few. The strongest one is of the odor and smoke from his cigars! Also, he wore his hearing aid device in the breast pocket of his shirt with the little wires going up the side of his face to his ears, giving him a rather odd look.

A quote from my brother John says it well: "We remember our grandfather Hal, or 'Pop' as our parents called him, as a cigar-smoking, rather intense person who used to jokingly say he'd 'sit on your ear' if we didn't behave!"[1]

Horace was the only son of John and Elida Langston, and he was born in Chicago, IL in 1887. He had a younger sister, Julia, born in 1891. Horace graduated from Oak Park River Forest High School in 1905.

At the age of 18 he began to pursue his love of photography, not choosing to follow in his father's footsteps in the printing business. He began his photography career in 1905. Over the years he had studios in Austin and Oak Park, and he specialized in children's portraits.

He was a member of the Lion's Club and Masonic Lodge for many years, but his major interest was in the Rosicrucian Fellowship, of which he was a member. This group of men and women embraced the "Christian Mystic Philosophy" which encompassed art, religion, and science. Their purpose was to spread the gospel and heal the sick.[2]

---

[1] John Roger Langston, grandson, ***The Langston Family and Heritage***
[2] ***The Langston Family and Heritage***

Family Life

Hal met **Hildur Lillian Christina Anderson**, born in 1889, in Oak Park, IL. They married in 1912. Her family had moved there from Omaha, Nebraska. They lived in the Chicago area, Austin and Oak Park also, for most of their married life. They finally settled in the home at 311 Elmwood Ave in Oak Park with Hal's parents, John W. and Elida Langston, and Hal's sister Julia. Several family members had stayed there over the years.

Soon after their marriage Hal and Hildur began their family. **Horace Ayres, Jr** (Ted) was born 2/8/1913, **Warren Reeves** was born 4/8/1914, **Wayne Anderson** was born 12/31/1915, and **John Gordon** was born 5/9/1917. **Roger Alan** came along five years later, 1/15/1922.

You may notice that it was the practice at the time to use family surnames as middle names for newborns. Ayres, Reeves and Anderson were three of those family names. Much later Uncle Ted would comment at a Langston family reunion that it would be a nice idea if that custom could continue. When Diana Boyce Wolff, daughter of Karen Langston Boyce, named her son Cody, she chose Langston as his middle name to honor Ted's request.

311 Elmwood Ave, Oak Park, IL

A home with five boys to raise would surely be a busy place, especially with the pranks the boys were known to play on each other. As teens though, they did try to help the family. Wayne relates that if there were a job available in the community, such as a paper route or delivery boy, whoever was the right age would be expected to take that job. Wayne had to quit high school to accept a delivery job at a cleaner's to help the family.[1] He later graduated after taking night school courses.

As the boys grew older they loved to bring their dates home and tease each other's girlfriends. On Sunday afternoons they would all gather at 311 and drink hot tea and eat cinnamon toast. Hildur would play the piano. Hal (Pop) played the mandolin, and Wayne played the steel guitar while everyone sang.[2]

After John W. and Elida passed away the family stayed in the home at 311 until sometime after the Depression when they lost the house to foreclosure. Pop, Hildur, Roger, and John went to live with Hildur's mother, Grandma Anderson. Wayne, Ted, and Warren had all married and moved on by then.

The Langston Studio

Ted and Pop opened the Langston Studios in Joliet on April 17, 1940. Pop and Hildur moved to the town of Lockport, near Joliet, to 1726 Hamilton Street. By then Hildur had found employment at the Boston Store where Ted had also worked, and he trained her to take over the photography department when he left to set up Langston Studios.

Their lives were just beginning to settle down when World War II began. Ted enlisted in the army, knowing he'd be drafted anyway, so Pop continued with the studio, assisted by his sister Julia, who did negative retouching, and

1726 Hamilton St. Lockport, IL

[1] Anecdote from Wayne A. Langston
[2] Memory of Ted's wife, Lydia Langston

son Wayne, while employed with Burton Holmes Films at the time, as bookkeeper.[1]

World War 2 would interfere with everyone's lives, as three of Hildur's and Pop's sons, Ted, John, and Roger, went off to serve overseas. Wayne was drafted and served stateside. Warren was not accepted in the draft but worked for a parachute company for his effort for the war. Fortunately, all three brothers came back alive and whole, and the family was reunited once more at war's end in 1945.

The Langston family had grown to include five grandkids. Most of them lived in Illinois in the Chicago area so they were able to gather fairly often. Although I was under 11 years old, I recall the house, the yard where we played, and the old stone wall where all the photos were taken. In the photo below Wayne, far left, and John, center, were still in uniform as the war dragged on..

From left: Ted, Warren, Wayne, Pop, John and Roger, summer, 1948

---

[1] ***The Langston Family and Heritage***

The Langston Studios, 1940 – 1952
65 E Jefferson St, Joliet, Illinois

A writeup in the <u>Joliet Herald News</u> in 1944 describes Hal (Pop) Langston as having "a style of photography which is distinctly individual as well as decidedly modern, so much so that his work is recognized everywhere."[1]

At right is a photo of a business card for the studio

[1] *The Joliet Herald News*, 1944

Final Years

After his retirement Hal became a stamp dealer and was also interested in astrology.

Sadly my grandparents did not live past their 60's. Grandma Hil passed away from breast cancer January 4, 1951, at the age of 61. Grandpa Hal followed the next year, December 29, 1952 at the age of 65. Their legacy has inspired the Langston family in several ways: to follow our dreams, to cherish our families, and to live life bravely and with faith.

Chapter Seven – John William Langston
4/9/1854 – 6/2/1925

John W. Langston, grandfather of Wayne A. Langston, was the titular head of the Langston clan at the turn of the 19th century. He was born in Sandusky, Ohio on April 8, 1854. He was the son of John and Margaret Weber Langston. John W. Sr. was born in England in 1831 and arrived in this country on Aug. 21, 1849. John W. Sr. died March 1, 1888.

The siblings of John W. were his younger brother Edward, and his sisters Elizabeth Jane and Alice.[1] The family moved from Ohio to the Chicago area before 1860 and settled in Oak Park, IL. John W's early years revolved around the church where he was recruited by a Mr. Moody who was establishing the Moody Bible Institute. At age 16, John worked at a printing company which is where he got his start and continued as a printer throughout his life.[2]

John met his future wife, Elida Ayres, in Quincy, IL. She was born in Keokuk, IA, the daughter of druggist Horace Hamlin Ayres and Julie Ann Reeves Ayres. Elida was living in Keokuk at the time, and John moved there and worked with the *Daily Gate City* newspaper until he and Elida were married on Feb. 25, 1880. They lived in a rented apartment before moving to Oak Park, IL.[3] John and Elida had two children, Horace, born 4/25/1887, and Julia, born 10/21/1891.

---

[1] *The Langston Family and Heritage*
[2] *Oak Leaves*, June 13, 1925
[3] *The Langston Family and Heritage*

John and Elida built the house at 311 Elmwood Avenue in Oak Park, which stayed in the family for many years. My father Wayne and his brothers often referred to it in the stories they told about growing up there.

John W. worked at several printing companies before starting his own, The Langston Press. He was also an active member of the community as the first President of the Colonial Club and a member of the Royal League of Oak Park. In 1901 he became a trustee of the town of Cicero and was the tax assessor of Cicero and Oak Park. He served as a trustee for the village of Oak Park from 1905 to 1907.

In addition to his career as a printer, John W. Composed music and wrote poetry. He wrote the music and lyrics of a love song dedicated to his wife titled, "My Sweetheart Elida." It was written and published in 1916.

Prior to that he published a songbook for children which he dedicated to the Porter Memorial Sunday Schools. It was a booklet containing six songs with a copyright by John W. Langston in 1906.

He also penned the poem, "George and His Young Axe," thus beginning the Langston tradition of writing poetry and limericks.

George and His Young Axe
The Langston Version

[Read by John W. Langston before the East End Men's Club, Oak Park, IL on the evening of George Washington's birthday, Feb. 22, 1898]

One restless boy,
One sharp-edged toy,
A most destructive combination.
On mischief bent
This couple went
To make hist'ry for the nation.

To orchard fair,
With fruit trees rare,
Where to grow, a cherry tree was battling;
With morals lax
George raised the axe
And 'swat' this tender sapling.

A little later
His irate pater
Bore down upon the scene.
With flashing eye
The sire drew nigh,
With searching look so keen.

Who hewed it down?
He cried with frown
What ruthless hand so mean?
The George confessed,
He could not rest
Before that stern set mein.

I cannot lie
The youth did sigh
As he explained the facts.
I struck the blow
That laid it low
To try my youthful axe.

My noble boy
It gives me joy
The father quick replied.
I'd rather be
Without a tree
Then know that you had lied.

SUPER
GRANDPA

Chapter Eight – Carl Oswald Hasdal
2/18/1887 – 12/26/1951

Carl Hasdal, father of Jean Hasdal Langston, immigrated to the United States as a young man in his twenties and led a very interesting life here. Even before that time he accomplished much in his home country of Norway. I was only ten years old when he passed, but I fondly remember him as my grandpa and enjoyed learning his history as I grew older.

Early Life in Norway

Carl was one of five children born to Tallak and Kristiane Olsen. He was the eldest, born February 18, 1887, in Risor, Norway. His siblings were Christian, Anna, Natalie (Nati), and Dagny. His father owned a butcher shop, but when he died in 1898 Kristiane was unable to claim payment from customers who owed them money. Due to lack of funds she was unable to raise all the children on her own. So, Anna and Nati were sent to separate families. Dagny remained home with her mother and the boys; Carl and Christian, were sent to live with their Uncle Andrew.

Standing: Dagny, Christian, Anna, Nati
Seated: Kristiana and Carl

One story from that time goes like this: As a teenager, Carl was a handsome, six-foot athlete who loved to ski and loved ski jumping. He won a ski jumping competition at Holmenkollen in Oslo, and the prize was a pair of jumping skis. However, his Uncle Andrew suspected that Carl had stolen the skis and made him burn them! This suggests their uncle apparently raised them with an iron hand.

By 1906 at the age of 19, Carl had already changed his last name from Olsen to Hasdal, taking the name from the area where his Uncle Andrew lived, Hasdalen. It was common at that time for people to take the name of a well-known person or place as their last name.[1] His brother Christian also changed his name but spelled it Hasdahl.

Sailing Career

Carl left Uncle Andrew's home while still in his teens and joined the merchant marines. He was a sail maker and later took training to become a First Mate. According to research done by John R Langston, grandson of Carl, for *The Hasdal Family,* Carl passed his examination for Standard Mate at age 19 on May 5, 1906, and sailed on the Bark *Chacma* for 22 months before taking his exam for First Mate.

After passing with flying colors on May 1, 1908, he boarded the *S. S. Brilliant* and sailed with it until Mar. 1, 1909. He then left the *Brilliant* to join the Norwegian Navy. His brief stint with the Navy ended on Oct. 19, 1910, after sailing with the Bark *Niola* as First Mate.

Emigration to America

In the early 1900's when Carl Hasdal emigrated, there were more individuals than families coming into America. Many people were settling in urban areas and forming close relationships with other immigrants or countrymen. Chicago was a common destination for many of those coming from Norway. and that is probably why Carl chose this city. His name was

---

[1] *The Hasdal Family*

found on the passenger list for the ship *Hellig Olav* out of Christianfjord (Oslo), Norway on Mar. 11, 1911.[1] He is listed as a 23-year-old male, single, a seaman, and a citizen of Mandal, Norway. His mother is listed as Kristiane Olsen, and he is shown to be heading to Chicago, IL.

Life in Chicago

Once settled in the new city, Carl found work in the painting and decorating trades. While researching his book, John Langston came across a recommendation from a Mr. Charles H. Hill which indicates that Carl had worked for him in Nov. of 1913.[2] Carl continued in that trade for many years.

Meanwhile, Anna Gunderson had emigrated to Chicago in 1907 at the age of 21. She worked as a domestic for a family there for two years and then, feeling homesick, she returned to Norway. Three years later, in 1912, she returned to America for good. She and Carl had met previously in Moss, Norway, and she met him again while working in Chicago. After a time they married, settled in Chicago, and started their family. Their first son, Carl Morgan, was born in 1915 and son Ralph in 1917.

A colorized version of an early photo of Carl and Anna

In 1918 the couple bought their first house in Oak Park, IL at 943 Division St. It was here that daughter Jean was born on Dec. 4, 1918. Their youngest daughter, Edith, was born in 1927.

Family Life in Oak Park

When the children reached school age they attended Horace Mann School across the street from their home. They had only spoken Norwegian at home, but the school insisted they speak only English while in class, so from then on Carl and Anna learned English along with their children, and that was the language they spoke at home as well.

Anna and Carl enjoyed a busy social life with their friends in the area. Many Norwegian immigrants had settled in the Chicago area at that

---

[1] Ibid
[2] Ibid

time. The Hasdals were members of the Lutheran Church, Jonas Lei Lodge, and the Sons of Norway. They enjoyed card games such as Whist and Pinocle, and of course Bingo.

While Carl was busy with his commercial painting, during his few leisure hours he painted oil landscapes of his beloved Norway. The flourishing sails of the ships in his seascapes tell the tale of his former life as a sailor. A self-taught artist, he had amazing talent. Several family members are happy to have some of hia artwork that has been handed down to them. Like those pictured below, they really are treasures.

Carl had decided to remodel the house in the early 1930's and he did most of the work himself. This included new siding, a fireplace with an electric burner in the living room, French doors between the front and back parlors, an enlargement of the back bedroom including a porch and railing, and a breakfast room which was under the back porch.[1]

[1] Taken from an interview of Jean Hasdal Langston by her son, John, 1988

Depression Years

When Jean was about 15, the family was forced to leave their home. The Depression hit, and Carl could not find work; he was a painter and decorator and did not work during the winter.

Money was scarce, and Carl even took down several of his paintings and tried to sell them. Their son, Carl Morgan, whom they called Morgan, quit school to find a job to help the family, but the money still ran out, as did the coal. They went to the court for help and were told to go to Legal Aid. At that time banks sold mortgages to individuals and payments were made one time per year, instead of monthly.

Ralph, Carl Morgan, and Jean

In an effort to help the situation, President Roosevelt introduced the Homeowner's Loan program, government bonds to help people avoid losing their homes. So Anna and Carl applied for one of these loans and called their mortgage holder to see if she would take a government bond. However, the woman who held the Hasdal mortgage did not like Roosevelt and forced Carl and Anna to leave their home.

They walked away without getting a penny for the house and there was a judgment against Carl which prohibited him from purchasing another property until he paid the mortgage penalty.[1] As they moved to an apartment in nearby Austin, they were determined to overcome this terrible experience and enjoy a good life with their children, the life they had dreamed of when they first arrived in the U.S.

One year later, on October 29, 1935, Carl and Anna headed to the courthouse again, but this time the occasion was one to rejoice. On that day Carl and Anna Hasdal, who had suffered the Great Depression like millions of others, became citizens of the United States.

The family now lived in a rental house on Iowa St in Austin, and this was the place for the wedding of daughter Jean and Wayne Langston in

---

[1] Ibid

1939. The newlyweds had several apartments after that and then moved to Skokie, IL.

They had three children in three years, Karen, Lloyd and John, and then in 1944 Wayne was drafted. Jean moved back with her parents at the Iowa Street house. After nine months in the Navy, Wayne returned and they became the renters. Jean's parents became the caretakers at the Norwegian Federation on Kimball Avenue. They lived in an apartment above the meeting rooms. Anna prepared meals for the members while Carl saw to the care of the building.

Their apartment was small but adequate, a place where Anna could enjoy her kitchen while Carl painted nearby. Here is where I have my earliest memories of my grandparents.

We children were sometimes allowed to play downstairs in the large meeting room when nobody was there. Grandpa was kind and playful; he sometimes put one of us on his shoulders or walked around the room doing a handstand. I remember hearing Cubs baseball games on the radio when we visited. Both Anna and Carl were Cubs fans; perhaps it was because the team won the World Series in 1908, around the time they came to Chicago. Grandma Anna was fond of riding the streetcar with her friends to go to Wrigley Field to watch Cubs games.

I remember the wedding of our Aunt Edy when I was a flower girl, and my mother Jean was a bridesmaid. My grandparents looked so special in their formal attire, and they were so happy for my aunt.

They are very serious in the photo at the right, but not so much in day-to-day life or when they were with family. They were always so good-natured and caring, and they loved having family over to visit. They adored all their grandchildren.

The Art of Rosmaling – Norwegian Rose painting

Besides the wonderful land and seascapes Carl painted, he did some lovely work on wood pieces using rosemaling patterns typical of Norwegian art. The photos below show a huge trunk that he painted which today is still owned by family.

Rosemaling is a type of Scandinavian decorative folk painting that flourished from the 1700s to the mid-1800s, particularly in Norway. It is practically a lost art today

Grandpa Hasdal was one year away from retirement when he died of heart problems in 1951 at the age of 64. He left us too soon but he made the most of his life as an immigrant coming to a new country. He will be remembered for that, for his wonderful skill in painting, and for the love and care he showed his family.

Important Documents

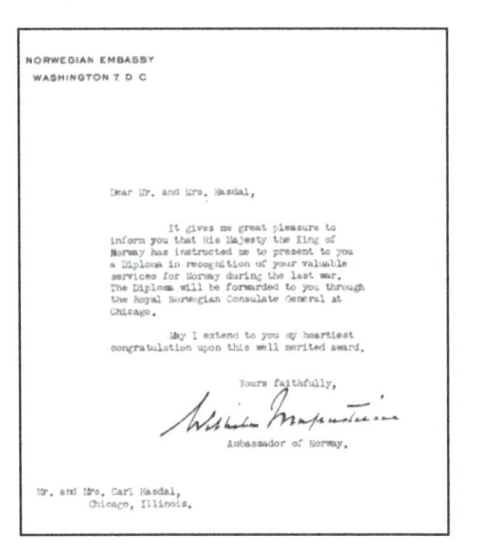

Above: Carl's Citizenship Document
At left is a letter from the King of Norway thanking Carl and Anna for their work during WWII, most likely with the Red Cross

blessed
GRANDPA

Chapter Nine – Tallak Olsen
12/16/1853 – 5/4/1898

Tallak Olsen was the father of Carl Oswald Hasdal (Olsen). He was born December 16, 1853 in the town of Risor, Norway. His parents were Anna Tallaksdatter and Ole Olesen. They lived on the small farm Kleven belonging to the farm Randvig. There is one family report that Tallak became a "sailship officer" before his marriage, but that cannot be confirmed.[1]

Tallak married Kristiane Olsen Risholt (born March 4, 1853) on July 14, 1881. They had five children: Anna, Carl, Christian, Natalie, and Dagne. They lived in Risor where Tallak owned a butcher shop.

There are two conflicting stories about Tallak's demise: from his son Christian's family it is told that Tallak died at sea from lung inflammation at the age of 38, and is buried somewhere in the Netherlands. This version came from the great-grandson of Tallak, Birger Heiberg, who lives in Norway."[2]

From left Tallak, Christian, Anna, Carl, Kristiane. In front Natalie and Dagne

The granddaughter of Tallak, Marguerite Johnson,[3] gave a different account told to her by Tallak's daughter Anna Olsen. She related that at age 45 Tallak became ill and spoke with each of his children, asking Anna, the eldest, to take care of their mother Kristiane after his passing. Tallak died at home 5/4/1898 and was buried in Risor. This version seems the more logical one.

---
[1] *The Hasdal Family*
[2] Ibid
[3] Daughter of Anna Olsen

After his passing one of his sisters wanted his business sold. Kristiane had to collect the money from the sale, and she sent daughter Anna, age 13, to do this. Because she was unsuccessful, the family had no money and had to move to Kristiane's hometown of Mandal where she hoped to get some help from her family there. Sadly, this did not work out either, and Kristiane was forced to send her children to new homes: Anna to Moss to work for her Uncle Hendrick, the boys Carl and Christian, were sent to live with Tallak's brother Andrew. Natalie was sent to live with a wealthy relative and Dagne stayed at home with her mother.[1]

Olsen Cousins Connect

Marguerite on the left, Jean at right

Two of the Olsen cousins reunited in St Charles, IL in 2004. Jean Hasdal Langston, the daughter of Carl Olsen Hasdal, and Marguerite Olsen Johnson, daughter of Anna Olsen, met at the Baker Hotel when our two families met for lunch. They hadn't seen each other in many years. Jean had recently moved to Illinois from Florida. Marguerite (Peg) was living at the Holmstad, a senior retirement facility, with her husband Larry. After their initial meeting they spent many enjoyable times together.

---

[1] Ibid

Closing Thoughts from the Author, Karen Langston Boyce

This is my second book, and I hope it will become a special one for everyone in our family. After writing the stories in the ***Grandma Book***, I couldn't wait to write the corresponding stories about our grandfathers.

Learning the personal history of the grandfathers in our family can give us a new understanding of them. The times in which they lived defined how they could structure their lives; whether they had the freedom to choose their life's work for example, or whether they were forced into whatever occupation came along. As a group they faced wars, the Great Depression, ill health and other stressors of the times, yet they all, as far as we know, kept their families intact and provided for them as best they could.

I believe that somehow the generations that preceded us have passed along a strength of purpose and a devotion to family that can be seen in each and every one of us today. We can honor them by following that unspoken tradition as we enjoy each day with our own families.

K.L.B.

Acknowledgements

Heartfelt thanks go to my brother, Josh Langston, for editing and publishing this memoir, and for his contributions to our family memories. As a fledgling writer I would have been lost without his help. My brother John, whose amazing efforts produced both the Langston and Hasdal histories, has also been very helpful to me. I so appreciate his input and encouragement.

Many thanks to my brother, Josh Langston, who guided me all the way and assisted in the editing and printing.

After all, this is a *family* memoir–it's for all of us, and those yet to come.

janda books

Made in the USA
Las Vegas, NV
01 April 2025